BIKE
TRAINING

The Ultimate Cycling Guide to Get
Fitter, Faster & Stronger Through
the Power of High Intensity
Interval Bike Workouts

By Dominique Francon

Disclaimer

The information provided in this book is designed to provide helpful information on the subjects discussed. The author's books are only meant to provide the reader with the basics knowledge of the topic in question, without any warranties regarding whether the reader will, or will not, be able to incorporate and apply all the information provided. Although the writer will make his best effort share her insights, the topic in question is a complex one, and each person needs a different timeframe to fully incorporate new information. Neither this book, nor any of the author's books constitute a promise that the reader will learn anything within a certain timeframe.

This book is for informational purposes only. You should always see your medical expert before starting any physical activity, or diet. By no means this book intends to replace the advice of a professional. Proceed at your own risk.

Table of Contents

Preview Of "Buddhism For Beginners! - The Ultimate Guide To Incorporate Buddhism Into Your Life – A Buddhism Approach For More Energy, Focus, And Inner Peace"

About the Author

Dedicated to those who love going beyond their own frontiers.

Keep on pushing,

Dominique Francon

Introduction
It's Time to HIIT the Road

Oh God, there's that hill again. Every day. It never gets any smaller, never gets any easier. It's always there, daunting, taunting, standing tall just to make me curse and sweat on my way home. That's it, the worst part of commuting downtown with my bike— it's not the traffic, it's that goddamn hill. And there's no way around it.

Does this inner monologue sound familiar at all? It might. City cyclists know all too well the troubles that come with the daily commute: cars that think they don't have to move to pass you, coming within an inch of taking off your arm and their side mirror in a single second; jaywalking pedestrians, thinking that because they can't see a car, the road must be clear; potholes that always seem more common (and deeper) on the sides of the road than in the middle; and, of course, the sheer physical difficulty of cycling for more than 30 minutes.

That inner monologue is one I used to say to myself every day coming home from work. I lived mid-town and worked downtown, and in my city, downtown is near the water—it's quite literally *down*town. Going into the office was a cinch, a leisurely stroll, more downhill than up. Coming home was another beast altogether—especially that one hill, right in the middle, on the cusp of the downtown border.

It was a *behemoth*. I never enjoyed it. Cycling is usually fun, but between the potholes and the traffic, staying straight was difficult enough on that sharp incline. I started taking side roads, but they weren't any less steep. There was simply no avoiding it.

Gradually, my calves and hamstrings strengthened up, and I got accustomed to the sensation of burning muscles that came with this everyday workout. It wasn't awful, but it wasn't particularly fun, and it always got my heart racing by the time I dredged myself to the top.

Then something changed.

I discovered a new system, a new way to cycle. It's more of a workout than a cycling style—a strength-building program, rather than a commute.

I started it by running, actually—it's more common in the running and weightlifting community than the cycling one. But it still applies, and a select few cyclists had begun adopting it both on the road and at the stationary bikes in the gym.

It's called HIIT—High Intensity Interval Training—and it's exactly what it sounds like. Cardiovascular researchers and professional runners, cyclists and bodybuilders have come together and come to an agreement: if you want to carve stronger muscles, burn more calories and train harder than ever before, you should be doing HIIT workouts rather than long, drawn-out ones.

So what is HIIT, exactly?

HIIT is what its name sounds like. It's a workout program that demands extremely intense workouts in short intervals, then resting for an even shorter amount of time. So you might go hard on a bike for two minutes, then rest for one, and repeat this eight times until you're so tired you've got to give up.

There's a lot of research that's gone into what makes HIIT workouts effective, and we'll explore that—along with specific workouts, supplementary diets and protein powders, and gym exercises—throughout the chapters of this book. For now, I want to finish my personal story.

After a few weeks of HIIT exercises, I found the hill that daunted me downtown got smaller. Or I got somehow faster. Or both. Anyway, I found it significantly easier to bike all the way home—I reduced the speed of my commute and made the whole process easier to handle. I didn't get any less sweaty, but the sweat got more manageable. The whole thing got way, way easier.

We do a version of this every time we do any physical exercise at all. Weight lifting, some scientists put forward, is a form of high-intensity interval training—extreme pressure followed by bouts of relaxation, and by the end you feel like you can't do any more.

When I was cycling up that hill, it was the same thing—only I wasn't doing enough reps to make it count.

HIIT isn't a replacement for long distance cycling, but it is an undeniably useful supplement, and makes for a great weekend workout. Pretty soon you'll find you're growing muscles you didn't even know you had.

So, if you're down to keep reading, flip this page over and let's talk more about where HIIT can fit into your cycling lifestyle. I think you'll be pretty surprised.

Chapter 1
HIIT Vs. Endurance (What They're Good For, Where They Fail and Why You Need Both)

Never let anyone tell you that what you're doing is wrong—even me.

The fact is, both HIIT and regular endurance training are useful in different ways. But they can be even more useful when combined.

Most people looking to burn fat and gain muscle mass—beefier arms, those elusive six-pack abs—will turn to HIIT and disregard endurance cardio entirely based on the assumption that cardio drains your muscles of their strength, because it makes them tighter and smaller.

Others think the opposite, because they want the opposite. Marathon runners don't want big, bulky muscles; they want lithe tight ones. Likewise, commuting cyclists tend to fall on the side of lighter and quicker bodies that can handle longer rides through the city. For them, biking isn't an exercise—it's a way to get from Point A to Point B.

The good thing about both is that they require very little extra equipment beyond what you've already got—cyclists need a bike, runners need running shoes, swimmers need trunks, and so forth. So if you're looking to lose weight, balance out those weekend drinks with some healthy activity, or just gain strength to tackle the commute more easily, you should know that you're on the right track.

First, let's more firmly define what we're talking about when we talk about the two forms.

Endurance training—sometimes called steady-state cardio, or long distance workouts—should be done at around 70 percent of your maximum strength output. Your heart rate will typically rise to about 120 or 150 beats per minute. With cycling it can be difficult to guarantee this—if you're going downhill, for example—but let's assume you're going at an even pace on a level road just for fun. Typically this lasts for around 30-60 minutes, depending on what you're doing.

HIIT isn't that—it's the furthest thing from fun. It should be done at maximum capacity—really, 110 percent—for a much shorter amount of time. Like, "less than two minutes" short. Rest for a certain amount of time (often when you're starting it should look like one minute of rest versus 30 seconds of workout; gradually you'll want to reverse those numbers) and then go again. The whole cycle shouldn't take longer than four or five minutes.

Whereas endurance training is aerobic, HIIT is anaerobic. Aerobic workouts require lots of oxygen and are made fat storages in the body. Anaerobic workouts are different, though—they rely more on carbohydrates, a staple of foods such as pasta, grains, rice, potatoes and fruits.

So which one is better?

Endure the cardio

Let's start by analyzing endurance cardio training. Aerobic training is critical to everyday life—in a sense, everything we do is fuelled by very weak outpouring of cardio activity, like walking, chewing and typing. At a more extreme level, all sports require cardio fitness—soccer and basketball are mostly running around for hours at a time. One of the reasons all athletes run is because aerobic training helps prepare them for anything and everything else.

Endurance training has been proven to be beneficial for our heart rates, too, which lowers the chances of us getting diabetes, strokes and heart attacks. Exercising too hard to fast (as in HIIT training) will cause your heart to beat so fast that the left ventricle, the one in charge of keeping hold of oxygenated blood before it spouts it out throughout the rest of the body, can't actually refill itself between contractions. Needless to say, that's not so healthy. It would be better to go at a slower, steadier rate, giving the heart enough time to allow the left ventricle to fill completely with blood. That gives us a lower heart rate, which is much healthier to consistently have—it goes along with being less stressed and more focused.

In other words, if you're prone to stress, HIIT might just stress you out *even more*. Which isn't to say you shouldn't do it at all—just that going slow and steady gives you a sort of appreciable work-down breather that will complement your regimen nicely.

Then, of course, there are critics of endurance cardio training. Some critics have some validity, but you should be wary of zealots too rigorously promoting one form or another. Some say endurance training will eat away at your muscles or give you weak joints—both are untrue. Your muscles may become smaller and tighter if you focus entirely and exclusively on cardio fitness, but they won't be eaten away—they'll still exist. And joints have actually been proven to be strengthened by cardio workouts, namely running and cycling.

There are, of course, many valid criticisms of endurance training: namely that it frankly doesn't build any muscle, which is what a lot of people strive for when they start. You don't get stronger by commuting to work by bike. You also don't burn as much fat by sticking to cardio training; even if your caloric burn is 500 per run, the actual act of running burns more of the day's carbs than stored fat.

It's also dangerous to train only one part of your body, because you heighten your chances of straining that particular muscle group.

HIIT it with your best shot

As a response to this, several trainers and exercise physiologists have developed the High-Intensity Interval Training method, meant to complement traditional workouts in every way.

HIIT can be anything—sprints, timed laps or biking up and down hills repeatedly. Professional athletes have long been timing themselves to get interval times as short as possible, which explains the scant fat on their bodies. But since the 1970s, and through to the '90s, several researchers from Sweden, Japan, the United States and Canada have found conclusively that interval training is just as useful to burn stores of fat off of everyday people as well—not to mention it being faster and more effectively than long distance cardio endurance.

The benefits are clear, and the consensus unanimous: HIIT is *the* single most prominent way to burn fat, no matter what exercise you're undertaking. The science behind it, in a very roughly defined way, is that your body continues to burn fat and calories even after you've finished working out—some call it the "*after burn effect*". When you push yourself as hard as you can, your metabolism stays heightened for hours after you've finished your workout. That means you're still burning calories and fat after you've finished working.

The other big boon to HIIT exercisers is the fact that it actually *builds* muscle. When we stress our muscles, we're enlarging them. That's obvious from bodybuilding. Since HIIT is such a strenuous type of activity, it actually transforms otherwise purely aerobic exercises like cycling and running into muscle workouts.

When we lift weights repeatedly and consistently, we build muscle. The same applies with HIIT workouts. Running as hard as you can may hurt the first time—okay, it may hurt *a lot*—but the benefit is that your muscles will grow and the pain will subside more quickly the more you do it. Soon you'll burn more fat than carbohydrates regularly, once your body has learned to save its carbohydrates for exercising.

All of this, in short, will make you stronger.

The third and last major benefit is how time efficient it is. Because HIIT workouts take only a few minutes (not counting the time it will take you to cool down and shower off, of course—you'll double the time doing all that), it's an ideal workout for busy on-the-go daytime workers. The results are measurable and very real.

Of course the negatives exist as well—mainly that the HIIT workout is a very specific workout plan aimed at building muscle, but not endurance. Obviously you can't fix your commuting or marathon troubles just by doing four minutes of exercise every two days, or even every day.

HIIT won't boost what aerobic exercise is good for: namely, muscles that can withstand high-stamina workouts and heart rates. Again, the bodybuilder comparison is helpful. A guy who eats 3,000 calories a day and spends two hours at the gym every day won't have a very high heart rate—he probably won't go running or even biking very often. He's big and strong, but can't endure the ongoing energy required to play, say, a full game of soccer—or a commute home from work on a bike.

And while the chances of straining a particular muscle may be slimmer than with cardio, you still risk straining your mind and entire body. Overzealous proponents of HIIT may find they have trouble sleeping and therefore focusing during the day. In short, you'll over-train—and possibly burn out quickly.

Why not both?

As with everything in life, the key to success lies in moderation. A little bit of Column A, a little bit of Column B.

Endurance cardio training is great for the long run (or long cycle), but ineffective with short-term gains. High-intensity interval workouts are great in the short term, but sticking with them exclusively can wear you out.

So... Why not both?

They won't counteract each other's properties, despite what some fitness websites will tell you. They actually complement each other.

If you're reading this book, I'm going to assume you already cycle at least a bit. If you're not on the bike at least twice a week, you should be. If you don't commute to work, then head out on weekends for solid 30- or 60-minute stretches at least. Get your aerobic heart rate going and get used to the feel of the bike. You want a steady resting heart rate, lower than most people's 60-100 beats per minute; aim for 40 or 50 to consider yourself "athletic".

Some professional athletic coaches also dissuade their athletes from doing HIIT training for longer than three months in a row, because of the toil it can take on their stamina. However, in the lead-up to a season, as well as at the end of an off-season, they'll ramp up the HIIT workouts to forge their players' bodies into peak athletic mode. But if they worked them that hard all the time? They'd be toast.

Some even recommend switching back and forth between three- or four-month-long workout stretches—three months of HIIT, three months of cardio. Doing both at the same time will stretch your body in different ways. You should focus either on aerobic exercise or muscle building, but one at a time.

Consider it a form of cross-training. Many cyclists will hibernate in the gym during harsh winters. Add on HIIT cycling to the winter gym months, rather than exclusively trying to compensate for your lack of distance by going long on the bike machine.

Really, the weather lends itself to this routine, especially if you're a cycling commuter. Use the mild spring and fall temperatures to work on cardio outside, and the frigid winter and sweaty summer months to work on muscular fitness. You'll best utilize all four times of year perfectly, and get stronger legs and faster speeds while you're at it. Honestly, it's a win-win.

Chapter 2
You Can HIIT on the Bike, Did You Know That?

I once read on a fitness message board that biking was the weakest form of cardio, and doesn't lend itself well to high-intensity interval training. Because biking primarily works the leg muscles, this poster argued, most of the body is left unscathed while only your calves, hamstrings and quads felt any real burn.

Let me clarify this for you, in case you read a similar warning: **that's bull**. Biking can be as strenuous a workout as you make it, and cycling is the only way to increase speed and strength on a bike—doing is working.

But other muscles are affected, too, if not necessarily stressed or built up when on the bike. We do actually use other muscles when we bike—simply by flexing our arms and gripping with our hands we're exerting some force of energy through our upper bodies. Our cores and abs need to be tight and strong to maintain a firm posture, our necks held high and straight.

And, most of all, any amount of workout will burn fat—and because you can't target which part of your body to reduce fat from, the fat will melt off automatically. You can do any HIIT regimen you want and the results will be fairly similar, calorie-wise; only the muscle gain will be in a different spot, obviously, depending on what muscles you use.

And really, that's one of the greatest things about the HIIT technique: the process can be whatever you want it to be. If you feel you can go harder for longer, you can work yourself based on fitness. If you're starting out and don't have as much time, do shorter bursts and you'll get just as much gain from it. Unlike aerobic exercise, it isn't the length that determines how much muscle you'll build or how much fat you'll drop—simply the act of extreme exertion alone will produce noticeable gains after a few weeks.

There are four main renowned HIIT regimens by four international physiological researchers. All of them can be adapted, but all have been prepared and tested in labs for their functionality. That said, they were also based on people running on treadmills—but can be easily adapted to biking, if you still pour out enough energy.

After these four, we'll go over some more biking-specific HIIT regimens, but to start it's useful to know what activities historically started this whole HIIT hype.

The HIIT Originators

Among the leading examples of HIIT techniques is the **Tabata regimen**, which was created by a Japanese trainer named Izumi Tabata in 1996 for Olympic speed skaters. It calls for 20 seconds of all-out extreme exercise, after which you're allowed to completely stop and rest for 10 seconds. After eight cycles, you'll hit four minutes even and feel as if all the air has been kicked out of your stomach.

The next one we'll look at is called the **Timmons regimen**, founded by United Kingdom native Jamie Timmons. This strategy is a lot like the Tabata regimen, but is a little more relaxed—though not much more. It likewise starts with 20 seconds of exercise at full speed, and then calls for two full minutes of lighter exercise—jogging or cycling at regular cardio speeds, rather than stopping completely for only 10 seconds. This process should be repeated three or so times. The Timmons is more ideal for those who are new to trying out HIIT in their lifestyles, and who might want to ease more fluidly out of their casual routines by leaving a part of it in. After a while, it's advisable to drop the casual speed and transition into something more hardcore.

If you want to focus on covering more distance rather than achieving faster speeds, then you might be interested in trying out the **Peter Coe regimen.**

This one was founded by Coe back in the 1970s, and began with sprinters running a 200-meter course as fast as they could. They were then asked to stop completely and relax for 30 seconds, only to turn around and run the 200 meters as fast as they could once again. After three or four times they probably couldn't do it any more. If you can find a stretch of safe and quiet road long enough to do this, then you're in luck; otherwise, set your stationary gym bikes for the 200 meters and clock how long it takes you to reach it.

The final and most recent contribution to this list comes from Martin Gibala, a Canadian teaching at McMaster University in Hamilton, Ontario. The **Gibala regimen** prefaces all workouts with three minutes of casual warm-up, followed by one full minute of, yes, you guessed it, 100 percent pounding exercise, then followed by a peculiarly specific set time of 75 resting seconds. This process is meant to be repeated between eight and 12 times. Because this is the longest lasting HIIT regimen, and the times are the longest of any of the four (both the intervals and resting times are on the longer side, as is the suggested number of cycles), it's not recommended that HIIT newbies or casual cyclists launch straight into this one. Take some time with one of the others before you feel you can tackle this.

The Way to HIIT Your Bike Specifically

Again, I need to stress: any of those above regimens can be applied to biking, even though they were more geared to running. Or else cyclists can enjoy the feeling of high-intensity interval running and still improve their cycling groove— cross-training is a proven way to increase strength and ability in any sport. That's why the Tabata method, the first and most common HIIT regimen, was created with running in mind, but geared for Japanese speed skaters. You can dabble around, mix and match the best from each universe.

But there are also specific biking workouts that can employ HIIT training. Finding a long, safe, quiet stretch of road is ideal if you need to do it on a real outdoor bike—just head out to the countryside for a bit. But because HIIT regimens are so brisk, and post-workout showers so immediately necessary, it is understandable that such a trip may not seem worthwhile. If that's the case, and the system doesn't suit you, then feel free to stick to the gym and adjust the stationary bike speeds and tension.

There are four cycling-specific HIIT workouts, ideal for burning fat and strengthening muscle mass. They all start the same way: with a casual ride for three minutes, with your heart rate pounding at around two-thirds of its maximum capacity. Some regimens are based on speed, others on distance;

in the end, they're all good, so choose which suits you best. (But don't go easy on yourself!)

The first is basically the Tabata regimen: 20 seconds of cycling as hard as you can, with ten seconds of stopped recovery, repeated eight or 10 times over. If you're on a mechanical stationary bike, set the tension to a high setting to challenge yourself, so you're not just going fast, but also hard. The difference between this and the Tabata running method is that the cycling twist calls for three minutes of warm-up and cool-down before and after the routine itself, making the whole process a much more involved biking experience.

The second method demands a faster speed and gives you more time to relax. After three minutes of warming up, aim for 120 rotations per minute (RPM)—basically ensuring you're doing two full wheel rotations per second. Try this for 30 seconds, and then rest for 30 seconds. If 120 RPM is too easy a speed, set a harder goal and shoot for that.

The third routine, much like the traditional Peter Coe regimen, is based on distance covered rather than speed cycled. Set your stationary bike (or find a route) for exactly one kilometer. Hit that kilometer in the fastest possible speed you can. Then relax and cycle along until your heart rate floats to around 125 beats per minute—a standard high cardio level. Then do the kilometer again, as fast as you can. Repeat this process five times.

The last one is unique to cycling, and is a terrific test for personal strength. Start by hitting 110 rotations per minute on the bike. (Again, this works best with stationary bikes in the gym.) Every 30 seconds, kick up the resistance on your bike a notch and try to maintain the same speed. Keep raising it every 30 seconds until you can't keep up to 110 RPM any more. Then cycle slowly for three minutes, and start all over again. Try this one three times for the most effective workout.

Alternative HIITs

Of course, you could also try a totally different routine. Make one up to suit your own needs. The first step is always to familiarize yourself with your body's maximum outputs and know your personal limits. If you want to try the Tabata method but need 20 or 30 seconds of rest after each interval, that's fine, provided that as time goes on you slowly decrease your rest time and increase your power time. Take it one week at a time, and gradually transition from 30-second breaks to 20-second ones, down to 10 seconds once you're comfortable.

Also, don't feel as though you have to do HIIT more than two or three times a week. In fact, especially as you're starting out, you really shouldn't do it so often, or else you'll risk injuring yourself.

Moreover, you won't see any measurable results in the first month, maybe even two—so don't even worry about that. Focus instead on daily or weekly goals. Take it slow and perform to the best of your abilities. Don't get dissuaded if you can't reach some goals immediately, because soon you'll be able to.

Obviously, for the best results, you should pair a weekly HIIT regimen alongside proper dieting (which we'll cover more of later on in this book) and a clearly focused mind.

So the next time you're at the gym and don't feel like pounding the iron, don't feel like you're wasting time by heading over to the bike machines. Take it slow at first, then go all-out. Remember: the beauty of HIIT is that it demands you perform to your own personal limits, whatever they may be. Don't look over at what someone else's speed is. You're in this for yourself, and yourself alone.

Once you've gotten a few months under your belt, you'll see the differences. You'll feel stronger. You'll have less body fat. You'll feel more lithe and agile, and feel lighter on your bike. Hills won't seem so daunting. Trust me: if you've started biking because you're trying to slim down, biking itself is only half the battle.

But with a bit of focus and determination, so much more is possible.

Getting Ready for HIIT

I had a friend once who didn't believe in the power or reliability of HIIT. Even though it's an objectively and scientifically tested method of exercise, this friend assumed it was rubbish, because he hadn't heard of it before. He hadn't tried it, and assumed that all exercise was alike—running was running, no matter what speed, and biking to work was better than walking, even if it was a light bike ride.

To this day, this particular friend won't join me in HIIT workouts, because he believes that if he's going to commit to a workout by putting on sports clothes, getting sweaty and hopping in the shower afterwards, the workout itself had better be at least 20 minutes long.

Don't let ignorance trap you into a certain belief pattern. This kind of thinking is old-fashioned, outdated and incorrect. There is a benefit to trying new things, especially because high-intensity interval training isn't supported by any single sect of people. There's no one trying to sell you anything, no necessary protein powders or diet pills. This is simply a regimen of exercise that many have found to work, but one which comes unnaturally to us when we think of exercise. But it really does work.

The best way to witness this transformation is to do it yourself. Experiential learning is always the best method.

With that in mind, I'd like to go over a few detailed weekly regimens. Assuming you don't already practice HIIT, we're going to start from the very beginning.

We can use the above regimens as a base, but we won't be able to achieve them off the get go. We need to build up to that level of skill.

But with a bit of focus and determination, so much more is possible.

Easing Into the HIIT Lifestyle

Okay, so we're going to start slower than what Tabata or Coe had in mind. We're going to start with more rest time than what they suggest, but as the weeks progress we're going to recalibrate the whole thing and wind up doing fully-formed HIIT workouts.

The following regimen is based on two-week patterns, because it's very dangerous to push yourself too fast too early. If you're absolutely certain that you can handle skipping ahead, obviously I can't stop you—but always consider your safety first.

Weeks 1 + 2: Do a lighter version of the Tabata workout. Reverse the times. The starting point to an extreme workout necessarily involves more rest time and less exercise time—we're talking 15 or 20 seconds of exercising as hard as you can, following by one full minute of rest. Try this very basic workout three or four times a week for two weeks. I'd generally recommend **Mondays, Wednesdays, Fridays** and optional **Saturdays** if you have the chance.

Weeks 3 + 4: Now we want to up the challenge. Now that your body is fully used to at least intervals of extreme exercise, you should maintain the same amount of rest—one full minute—but up the exercise portion to 30 seconds. Again, stick with three or fours days a week.

Weeks 5 + 6: Now it's time to really push yourself. Now that you're used to cycling up to 30 seconds as hard as you can, lessen your rest time: try giving yourself only 30 seconds, down from that full minute. Now you'll be resting as long as you'll be cycling. Note that "*rest*" in this instance can mean either slowing your speed to a casual one or stopping completely; do whatever feels more comfortable depending on how exhausted you feel at the time.

Weeks 7 + 8: This is the final home stretch. Now you'll need to rest for only 15 seconds at a time, and still cycle for a solid 30 seconds. Your body will be so used to exerting all its energy at once that the 30 seconds of workout will feel like a snap, and hopefully the rest will be enough to calm you down.

HIITing Beyond the Bike

Let's say you're sick of biking—you commute every day with it, and you don't feel comfortable riding unless you're going a long distance. That's fine; I get that.

The good news is that you can cross-train with any of the above HIIT regimens from the previous chapter that you like. Actually, it's probably a good idea—any HIIT regimen will ultimately strengthen your muscles and make you faster and more in control of your own body, which will in turn improve your cycling prowess.

So consider cross-training by doing HIIT on your legs or in a swimming pool instead of on the bike. As a bonus, you'll be working different muscles, which, while not especially useful for biking per se, will still give you a more nicely overall toned body.

Consider substituting the above workout—the one from this chapter—with running or swimming instead of biking.

Or, if you'd prefer, you can try this popular variation on the Tabata method, which is totally achievable at home and requires a bit of space wherever you can find it. The key to the following regimen is to do it *as quickly as you can*—not just the individual workouts, but without leaving any space in between (beyond the 10 seconds of allocated rest time).

1. **Fast Feet**: Jump-step up and down in one spot as quickly as you can, kind of like a quick and miniature form of jogging. Do this for 20 seconds as *absolutely quickly* as you can. Then rest for 10 seconds. Then do it all again—20 seconds of fast feet (also sometimes called "pitter patter") and 10 seconds of rest. This is great for getting calves and quads burning.

2. **High Knees**: Like Fast Feet, this one requires consistent leg movement—large, exaggerated steps wherein you lift your knees up past your hips. Again, to do this properly in the style of HIIT, you've got to

do this as absolutely quickly as you can. Your legs should hurt. You should want to give up. Do it for 20 seconds, then give in to 10 seconds of rest; repeat again.

3. **Mountain Climbers:** Same deal, 20 seconds of intensity followed by 10 seconds of rest. Mountain climbers are great for working arm and core muscles—again, better for overall health than for pure cycling strength. If you're unfamiliar with the terminology, *"mountain climbers"* are simply the exercise performed when you're in push-up position with your arms outstretched, and pull in one of your knees to your chest (or as close as you can come), then push it back out into the original position and switch legs. It should feel sort of like jogging in the push-up position.

4. **Burpees**: There are a few variations of burpees out there, and it's easy to get the process wrong. Push-ups are optional, but the push-up position isn't; from there, hop your legs up into your chest and shoot upright, then quickly jump up. Try to distinguish each jump—rather than making it one fluid motion from push-up to leap, first plant your feet firm and then straighten your back and leap up. Then fall back down into the push-up position. This is

a truly exhausting exercise, but the important thing is to maintain proper composure while doing it, even if you're doing it at top speed.

There are other exercises we can do, also, which we'll expand on in the next chapter: ones that don't involve the bike, but which can improve your strength and complement HIIT training very nicely. Don't feel like you have to constrain yourself to any single workout regimen; try a few and see what works for you.

But at the same time, don't give up just because one doesn't work immediately—it should be hard at first. That's the whole point. By the end of any HIIT workout, you should feel devastated, exhausted and unable to go on. That's good: that means it's working.

Chapter 3
The Science of Cycling: Physiology, Biology and the Human Body

Training isn't just an arbitrary thing—it's a science. There are rules and numbers to live and work by. And you don't always need a machine to help tell you what your numbers are, if you're in tune enough with your body, or know how to calculate what's going on inside.

Before we get ahead of ourselves, there are a few numbers to keep track of during this training process. One is heart rate, which you can develop through consistent cardio exercise, and the other is VO2 max—a somewhat nerdy way of describing how much oxygen you can use in a minute.

We'll start with VO2 max. Casual bikers don't tend to know their VO2 max, partly because it's more of a racing term, and partly because it's difficult to find without a machine and physiologist or trainer at your side. Typically, in order to find your VO2 max number, you'll have to pound through on a stationary bike that increases its pace until your body physically falls apart—while you're struggling, a physiologist would measure how much oxygen you're using by strapping a mask onto your face and recording your breaths.

While VO2 max is often judged in liters, sports athletes use a more precise mathematical equation: milliliters of oxygen per kilogram of body mass per minute. That allows for a more precise reading of an individual's output. So whereas an average person's VO2 max sits around 40ml/m/kg (AKA for every kilogram of their body, they exhale 40 milliliters of air per minute), a highly trained athlete may achieve a VO2 max of 80ml/m/kg or higher.

How do you increase your VO2 max? You need to learn to use your oxygen more efficiently. Some lucky buggers have naturally larger than average lungs, but even those with normal-sized ones can increase what nature gave them.

The good news is that VO2 max training directly coincides with HIIT. Interval training is one of the best ways to increase body functions in any capacity—and the amount of air you can take in during a single minute of riding hugely affects speed and endurance.

Before doing interval training of any sort, it's useful to know your VO2 max power level and your threshold power level. Many professional cyclists judge these outputs in terms of energy output as discerned by wattage. There are apps for this stuff (more of which you can read about in chapter 6 of this book), or you can use common numbers for a rough at-home calculation. The bottom line is that your VO2 max number will be based on two different tests, and you'll need some basic understanding of how your body functions athletically before beginning.

Your VO2 max power should be based on however many watts you exert by going for five minutes at a pushing, but doable, maximum power. Your threshold power is based on the wattage you exert during 30-minute bouts of maximum power, typically at 85 percent of your maximum possible intensity. Go hard, but don't push yourself over the edge. And rather than calculating one based on the other in theoretical terms, try calculating them individually by actually doing the exercises and recording this—this way, you know exactly what you're dealing with.

Maximizing Your VO2 Output

Here's an easy interval routine that should take just under an hour to complete. First off, every interval routine should begin with at least 10 minutes of warming up. Then, much like in a HIIT routine, you want to start by shooting into two full minutes of VO2 max intensity cycling—remember that the difference in energy output shouldn't destroy you by the end of the interval, but you should definitely be pushing yourself. Follow this up with around eight minutes of threshold-level intensity, and subsequently 10 minutes of lolling around to relax yourself and get some air back in. Then, repeat the process: two minutes at VO2 max, eight minutes at threshold-level, followed by 10 minutes of cooling down.

When you're done the exercise, you may feel like you can keep going even longer. Go ahead—feel free to change this routine up to add as much low- or high-intensity riding as you wish, if you want to make the most of your time on the bike. But it isn't necessary. Treat this routine as you would a bare minimum, a skeleton from which to work upon. Just don't forget to rehydrate and grab a few calories to pack inside.

What does this regimen do, you might ask?

First of all, it helps to increase your VO2 max. Those first two minutes activate your aerobic system, which helps you perform to your maximum capabilities. But when you drop to threshold levels, you're continuing with the same maximum oxygen intake and output, but without the overflowing lactic acid developing in your muscles. Basically, this means you're pushing your body straight into its maximum aerobic output condition without constantly pushing your muscles into suffering mode.

It's also a useful training regimen if you've never done HIIT before—this is a longer, more common sort of cycling interval training regimen that can lead into more higher-intensity intervals with less downtime, which is ideal for building strength. A high VO2 max is less helpful for pure strength output than it is endurance and adjusting your body level to perform at a quicker, more agile pace.

If you're racing often, or plan to enter your first race soon, longer interval training also has the advantage of simulating, to some extent, the race atmosphere—rarely do cyclists perform at top speed for the entire time, but you should be comfortable being able to reach up and grab that speed when it's necessary, while still enduring the rest of the race at a fairly intense speed.

Get that Heart Rate Going

Next, before we tackle any proper HIIT training, we need to discuss how to get a high heart rate. You'll need to adjust your muscles if you haven't been using them much.

That means, yes, you have to start with *cardio*. You've got to run, bike or swim consistently for at least two months for twice a week before you start HIIT. There are serious consequences otherwise: you might really endanger yourself when it comes to personal injury and straining muscles. You've got to ease into this.

If you're already a cyclist, that's perfect. Make sure you're on your bike for a solid 30 minutes a day at least twice a week (more is fine, of course, especially if you're a commuter), and if you've been going at a steady pace for most of the time, then focus on upping your speed if you can—push yourself harder than you'd normally go. You won't drastically cut down your time—maybe by a few minutes, but that isn't the point. The point is that this will force you to push your muscles more than what they're currently used to.

If you'd like to cross-train with running, and are not currently a runner, then start based on how much time you can manage. Don't push yourself to finish a 5k on your first outing. Go for as long as you can and then come home. After your first two or three weeks, you'll notice your body gradually getting used to the feeling of that aerobic pressure.

But you should definitely be at least comfortable with long distance cycling before starting hit regardless of whatever cross-training you want to try out. If nothing else, you'll need to acclimatize yourself to the feeling of being on a bike.

After a month of solid cardio, up the number of times per week you do it to three or four. Five and six a lot, and seven is absurd—when you're working out, you need good solid rest days. Rather than increasing distances, work on increasing speeds—try to do a 5k route faster rather than jumping to a 10k route. This is again because you'll need to ease your body into the feeling of pushing itself harder than what it's used to.

Endurance Lies in the Blood

Many are surprised when they discover that endurance depends as much on blood flow as it does on muscle and lung capacity. Blood is what moves oxygen around the body—it's great if your muscles are tight and strong, but without oxygen feeding them constantly while you ride, they're kind of useless.

The two big issues surrounding our bloodstreams are how much oxygen each cell can carry per minute, and how much blood you have to go around. They're interrelated, of course, but nevertheless distinct issues.

How much oxygen our blood cells can carry depends on your levels of hemoglobin, which in turn relies on the amount of red blood cells in your system. On average, men have 46 percent red blood cells, and women have 40 percent—but athletes across the board have averages several percentage points less, because endurance training literally changes the human physiology.

It's called "athletic anemia"—basically, what it means is that athletes' blood is diluted by higher amounts of plasma than what is normal in a human body. More plasma (recall high school biology, now: blood is made of up red blood cells, white blood cells and the liquid-like plasma through which it all floats) means more movement; move movement means more useful oxygen.

Athletes often also enjoy a higher number of red blood cells—though it's not enough to bog the plasma back down. It just means that endurance athletes have more blood cells flowing around more freely through their veins. For muscles, this is excellent. But when athletes stop training, their blood can quickly go back to normal—that's why casual exercisers don't enjoy this blood advantage unless they train hard often.

But there was one more aspect to blood levels, if you recall from an earlier paragraph—not just how much oxygen each cell can carry, but actually how much blood your body generates.

This varies wildly from person to person, though many natural athletes find they just automatically have more blood flowing inside them than most regular humans. Good for them. If you're not among the lucky, however, you can increase your blood levels by cardio and endurance exercises, although only within an understandably human amount.

An average man weighing 75kg would have maybe six liters of blood in his system. Exercise can raise this level up to 6.5 or seven liters. But some athletes naturally have up to nine or 10 liters pumping through their system—and the more blood you have, the more oxygen you can collect and move through your body.

If you want to raise your blood levels, in addition to interval and endurance training, you've got to focus your diet on it. Iron is fundamental to the creation of hemoglobin, and can be found in red meat, organ meat, beans, leafy greens and raisins. Folic acid and vitamin B12 are also useful in increasing your red blood cell count.

Lowering that Lactate

If you've heard the phrases "lactate" or "lactic acid" before, but never fully understood them, then let's take a minute to go over it.

We burn calories from one of two sources: they're either fat or carbohydrates. Carbs burn more commonly. When we break down carbs in their stored body form, known as "glycogen," our muscles produce a seepage of lactic acid. This acid flows through our bloodstream, releasing lactate throughout, which actually breaks down our muscle strength and slows us down.

This contributes greatly to what we know as short-term fatigue. When we work out, we're burning mostly stored carbs, which, after some time, makes our muscles feel weaker. Under normal circumstances, our bodies have no trouble dealing with lactate levels—it's when we produce higher than normal quantities that things start to go awry.

If you want to avoid a quick lactate build-up during sprints and climbs, look no further than the topic of this book: yes, once again, HIIT comes to the rescue, saving our bodies from lactate by transforming the way our muscles work in conjunction with the rest of ourselves.

Interval training with short bursts rather than long, sloping race-like rides are the best way to adjust your lactate levels and make your body used to the fact that this is how it can operate. Short but high-intensity intervals replicate peak racing conditions and help your bloodstream and muscles overcome those bursts of lactate regularly.

Fat or carbs? Why Not Both?

A key goal for those just starting to work out their bodies is to "burn fat"—a highly misleading suggestion, and arguably the most ineffective statement in the healthy-living glossary.

Anyone who knows about nutrition knows that fat is a healthy and natural byproduct—that is to say, when it is, actually, healthy and natural. Manufactured fats and sugars are far more harmful when taken in extreme doses, such as when they're condensed in a Hershey's chocolate bar.

When we ride our bikes, we're not actually burning fat. Not immediately. Our bodies first have to eat through the carbs of the moment—that glycogen that I mentioned just a few paragraphs earlier. While some amount of fat is needed and burned with every ride we take, we need a certain amount of carbohydrates to sustain longer rides. The amount of carbs we burn depends on a number of factors, including the intensity and duration of the exercise.

Carbs, you see, are stored in our muscles and liver and glycogen, and in our bloodstreams as glucose. If you're keeping well fed and athletic, you might have up to 2,000 kilocalories of these carbohydrate forms in your body, which—while it sounds like a lot—is really very little. Roughly 75 percent of this is stored in our muscles.

But when we're exercising for a long time, our glucose and glycogen levels start to deplete. When that happens, we're running exclusively on stored fat supplies. That's why, before a long race or running marathon, you'll find people packing away hearty carbs for energy storage—but we'll deal more with that in chapter 7.

If you're burning 3,000 or 4,000 kilocalories on the road, you're likely only getting half of that energy from glucose and glycogen. If you're trying to keep a strict low-carb diet, you won't be able to go anywhere near so far as to burn that caloric amount—you'll collapse pretty quickly. Burning fat stores is all well and good in the short term, but when gunning for greater distances and endurance, carb-loading is key.

But the good news is that, when you're keeping athletic on the bike, your body is able to store greater amounts of carbs while rationing them smartly, over a regular Joe who would simply eat some white bread and sit on the couch for the rest of the day.

Our Bodies, Our Lives: How to Measure Our Energy Impact

There are so many ways of measuring our energy exertion—we'll discuss one big way, the Borg Scale, in the next chapter, when we discuss the importance of energy exertion on the bike.

For now, I want to put one last cherry on top of our discussion of the body in relation to cycling. A lot of these facts may be obvious to some readers— others may find it too scientific and boring—but, ultimately, this is important to understanding how and why we cycle the way we do, and how we can get better.

Here are a few ways of measuring intensity that don't involve the external scales, but simply understanding our own bodies. These methods relate to systems of the body: our heart rates and our energy outputs. Our heart rates are tightly linked to our cardiovascular systems, whereas energy is derived from muscles pedaling quickly.

When we talk about body systems, we're talking about nervous systems, vascular systems or muscle systems—whole entities that comprise certain elements throughout our entire body, not isolated in a single space.

One such system is the muscular system. Muscular systems are gauged in watts, wherein power is determined by work divided by time. In this measurement, work would translate as gear size, and time becomes cadence—meaning that power rises when gear size increases, but cadence stays the same. In other words, as power output increases, race velocity rises as well.

However, chief among these bodily systems is the energy production system, the bodily system that delivers fuel to our muscles by way of digested proteins, fats and carbohydrates. Once brought to our muscles, this becomes ATP—adenosine triphosphate in the technical terminology. This happens no matter what kind of exercise you're taking part in.

If you're engaging in aerobic exercise, like a breezy ride, you'll be relying first and foremost on fat and putting carbohydrates second. The slower we pedal, the more fat we burn, and the more carbs stay in our body. (At a certain point in a long distance, the body will want to preserve those fats, and switch to carbohydrates—and only after it's depleted those will it go back to "burning fat," whatever that really means.)

When it comes to HIIT, though, you'll find yourself burning more carbs more quickly. Simply increasing your pedal speed and RPM actually turns cycling into an anaerobic exercise, meaning you're able to receive less oxygen than you need in order to function at the intense level you want. This creates ATP anaerobically, which calls for more carbs than fats.

From here, we've gone over what happens in this chapter: as carbs are turned into ATP, lactic acid is released into our muscles, which makes us tired and achey. This gets carried through our bloodstreams and turned into lactate.

Regardless of your mode of energy production— whether it's aerobic or anaerobic—lactic acid is inevitable. And therein lays the key to measuring our own energy outputs.

How is this possible? It's because we're constantly producing lactic acid—even right now, as I write this and you read it, we're both producing lactic acid, although at a level that is admittedly easy to control.

So it's only when we produce too much lactate that we feel the difference. That means it's possible for an athlete (or, more likely, his or her coach or personal fitness trainer) can determine a quantitative level of exertion.

This is possible in any number of ways. The first and easiest is by judging our lactate thresholds. When we overwhelm our lactate thresholds, we're crossing that line from lactate that's easy for our bodies to control, into lactate that makes us feel heavy and tired, which is what makes it accumulate within our bloodstreams. It's possible to pinpoint, with some degree of measurable accuracy, the moment at which our physical exertion causes us to cross this lactate threshold and start to lose our momentum. You'll feel it after going a certain distance, rising to a certain intensity or climbing a certain hill—you'll know it, and you'll feel it.

You can also use straight-up physiological improvement as a means of judging how fast you're going, or how much energy you have. By tracking your own bodily changes and improvement in speed and strength, over time you can get a strong idea of your racing fitness. Generally speaking, the faster you can ride, or the more intense your workout can get without producing as much lactate, the better your fitness will be for endurance racing.

You should also try measuring how smoothly you can pedal. Smooth pedaling means less lactate—it should be an easier movement than a grueling, difficult slog where each push pushes out more lactic acid into your bloodstream. Less effort means less lactate, which means you'll be able to go smoother for longer.

When it comes to that last note—smooth pedaling—having the most physically economical gear helps a lot. Saddle heights and handlebar raises can allow you to ride much farther and smoother without as much lactic acid exertion, and alleviate a lot of unnecessary stress from your muscles.

You can also judge how quickly your lactate levels return to normal by taking a recovery interval to time how quickly your muscles recover from their stressed out stage.

At the end of the day, the ultimate decider when it comes to judging your own lactate levels is pure experience—being out in the field, or on the bike machine, and being able to gauge, without any tools, how depleted your energy levels are. You don't need an extremely expensive piece of equipment to be in tune with your own body; people have been doing it, successfully, for generations before us.

So even despite the availability of lactate analyzers and smartphone apps, it's easier and more personal productive if you learn your own limits. This will enable you to understand your body better and feel more confident when it comes to approaching your actual limits—not your mental breaks that make you think you can't go on, but real, honest limits of your muscle capabilities. We all have them—and they're much further off than we tend to think they are.

But there's one more system to go through—the cardiovascular system. This ties in with the previous system, in that it relies heavily on lactic output and understanding the flow of our bloodstreams.

Heart rate monitors are common now among smartphone users and gadgetry fans. It isn't a proper gauge of speed, but it can shed light on your energy output—it's possible to exert all your energy just to maintain your current pace without increasing your speed at all.

But I'll refer to a new concept, the lactate threshold heart rate, as a determiner of a cyclist's ability. These thresholds differ from one athlete to the next—one may have a lactate threshold heart rate that kicks in at 80 percent of his maximum heart rate, whereas another finds it at 90 percent. This makes any objective, uniform calculation basically invalid. But if you compare two athletes who are operating at their maximum thresholds, then it's even—regardless of what else their body does to make it happen.

That's what makes this lactate threshold heart rate, or LTHR, so useful. While it does require precision to find, it's possible to do it fairly simply. Wear a monitor during a time trial—any trial at all, regardless of distance or company. All you need is an average heart rate, which you can use a predictor of your LT, and the following equation: divide your average heart rate by 1.05. That's it.

So, say you're running 10 miles, and your average heart rate might be 176. Divide 176 by 1.05 = 167. That means 167 is your LT.

See how easy that was to do without a fancy device or intense computational calculation? See how easy understanding your lactate levels can be? Really, that's the message I want to drive home in this chapter—that in order to strengthen and speed up our bodies, we have to get in touch with them. It's immeasurably helpful to understand your body's limits, movements, strengths and weaknesses.

Once you have a grasp on that, you're ready for the next step.

Chapter 4
Think You Know How to Cycle? You Have No Idea

There's an old insult for amateur cyclists: they're called "mashers," because they mash their feet up and down, instead of moving their feet in smooth circles, which allegedly utilizes the upward muscle motion of pedaling more.

This whole concept has been debunked long ago. Moving our feet in circles is tremendously difficult and counter-intuitive. When pedaling, we push down—the beauty of bike mechanics is that pushing down also pushes the other side up. You don't need to focus on exerting effort on somehow pulling up your pedals on an upswing; it's awkward, if really possible at all.

This is just one example of former "conventional wisdom" in cycling that's been debunked. A lot of recent studies have proven that cycling, as much as it is a complex sport that involves hardcore enthusiasts timing heart rates and red blood cell counts, is also fairly easy—especially if you're new to it.

But I must apologize: contrary to what this chapter implies, there are no real "secrets" to great cycling or improvement. Online regimens and dietary paths are common among at least some cyclists, and much of what's written in this book can be found elsewhere.

In an earlier edition of this book, some critics blasted me for not having offering them all-new information. That's because no information is new, really—what we know about riding a bike has only come from those who preceded us. There is no singular "right" way to cycle (as proven by the fact that neither HIIT nor long distance training alone can be a catch-all method to improvement), nor are there any magic formulas; there are only effective training systems that coaches and trainers have developed over years.

Beware the Overtraining Plague

Have you ever been so tired that you didn't want to continue? It doesn't even have to be biking—maybe you were hiking a mountain or running a marathon. This block—often more mental than physical among amateurs, although helpfully the opposite among more intense athletes—plays a huge role in determining how well we perform when called upon.

And the fact is, logically, very few people perform at their peak when they're tired.

Overtraining is a serious issue among aspiring athletes. It's known as "chronic fatigue," and is a clear symptom of overtraining, not taking enough rest days, and muscle over-exertion.

When riders enter into difficult workouts feeling energetic and full of pip, even if they haven't trained the previous day or two, they perform better. This immediate stress doesn't affect their muscles or cardiovascular system—when the time comes, your body knows what it needs to do.

Old and Unconventional? May Still be Effective

Here's an old training exercise from a 1946 edition of *Bicycling Magazine.* (Remember what I said: it's not a matter of magically new information, just a combination of previous knowledge.)

Grab your bike off the ground and speed walk with it, not letting the bike touch the ground. The trick is that you should contort your shoulder so that the cross bar isn't touched, but is lined up nearby.

This position forces you to throw your shoulders back and stretch out your chest and lungs. This encourages a strong grip, which in turn strengthens the smaller muscles in your wrists and arms.

Take Your Pick: Frequency, Duration, Intensity

There's an old adage in sports training that a workout involves three aspects: frequency, duration and intensity. You can focus your workout on any one of these, but working on all three at once (as in, trying to set a personal record in each) is mind-bogglingly difficult, and a surefire way to lead to overtraining and chronic fatigue.

Frequency is determined by how often you train—typically, non-athletes gaining momentum in the field would train between three and five times a week, while more serious or professional athletes work twice a day or more. Note that working out twice a day won't benefit you significantly—when you're at that level of peak fitness, you can only improve your game by small amounts.

Don't feel bad for needing to take rest days often, especially if you're working on high-intensity workouts, which HIIT enthusiasts will be. Rest days are natural and healthy, and going more frequently—as in, seven days a week—won't improve your body if you're not used to training that hard. Start slow, and build as per your own physical abilities.

Duration is another finicky one when it comes to HIIT workouts. Obviously, methods like the Tabata and Coe demand quick, short bursts on the bike, and don't need to be involved in longer durations than a few minutes.

Focusing on duration, or distance, is important if you're training for a long bike race or time trial, but not if you're going casually to burn a few calories and improve your commute. It's more important to focus on the energy you exert during a ride, rather than the length of the ride itself—you won't see much improvement if you ride a casual 40km in five hours, but if you do that same distance at 80 percent of your maximum potential speed, you'll feel it much more.

So, lastly, that leaves us with intensity. That's what I am encouraging you to focus on in this book. By focusing on hardening your intensity, you can build strength and grow larger muscles, making riding your bike over hills and overtaking competition much easier.

Obviously, all three components are necessary for healthy biking—I would never endorse anyone to rely exclusively on one aspect of exercise and neglect the rest. But for the purposes of this book, and incorporating HIIT training into your cycling routine, intensity tends to be at the forefront of these pages.

Judging Your Intensity

The big question remaining, then, is how to judge your own intensity. How does one know when they're at 85 percent versus 90 percent? There are smartphone apps, of course, and gadgets aimed at measuring your heart rate, blood flow and speed.

But there are also old-fashioned ways, and one of the truest and oldest methods is called "perceived effort." If you take this into account and spend a few months—well, years, really—honing this skill, then you should be able to accurately judge your own intensity on the fly.

You can calculate your own perceived effort by using the Borg Rating of Perceived Exertion Scale, which measures physical exertion on a sliding scale measures in Rating of Perceived Exertion, or RPE for short. In a scientific setting, this allows labs to accurately measure lactate thresholds and oxygen intake based on feelings alone.

The Borg Scale, quickly, ranges from 6 to 20, where 6 is a lack of physical exertion and 20 is the max. You judge your own level of physical energy exertion based on that scale, and, after a while of training, you can accurately determine how much energy you're putting into various activities, or activities at various times.

A key to the Borg Scale's success is self-honesty. You have to know your absolute limits and work down from there. Anything between 6 and 9 is considered very light exercise, whereas anything between 10 and 12 is somewhat light, and difficulty begins around 13. After 14, the difficulty increases until maximum exertion is reached at 20. Typically, a 12 or 13 might be walking around at an average pace for a long period of time—the difference between walking from one room to another, and walking 20 minutes to the store.

Chapter 5
Working Out Beyond the Bike - Let's Build Some Muscle

Remember the old adage: a team is only as strong as its weakest member.

Now put that adage into the context of the human body: a person is only as strong as their weakest muscle.

Cycling is a peculiar cardio exercise because it very specifically targets only certain muscles in the body, pretty much entirely in the legs. That's why it's so important for cyclists to do other workouts, too, beyond simply cycling. It's hugely beneficial to build strong core and shoulder muscles to balance your entire body. You don't necessarily need beefy arms, but in fact all core workouts work our arms to some extent anyway, so you'll notice some side effects there.

There's any number of deciders that factor into speedy cyclists, but one thing is certain: the strength and condition of muscles, tendons and tissues ranks high among them.

Of the human body's 660-plus muscles, cycling may not stress each one, but having as many in peak condition will improve cycling performance without a doubt. Stronger muscles, simply put, encourage a cyclist (or any athlete) to use as much force as possible—and while many cyclists focus on lithe speed alone, force, or strength, is equally important. Not only will increased strength improve race times, but it will lessen the chances of incurring an injury on the road, especially if those roads are uphill.

If you're worried about gaining weight through strength training, don't fret—the force you exert on the bike will more than make up for the added mass on the bike. (Although, that said, in most cases cyclists don't even gain that much weight by focusing on strength training for part of the year—many, in my experience, tend to believe that excess weight gained during the winter months is a result of strength training, when really it's simply a result of burning fewer calories, commuting by means other than cycling, and eating more. By the time cycling season starts back up, those added pounds will almost certainly disappear.

One of the benefits of strength training, particular weight lifting, is an improved lactate threshold—a significant aspect in determining your on-bike performance. Without weight lifting, we're using the same quick-acting muscles to produce a high amount of lactic acid. Strength training alleviates this risk by lowering your blood levels of lactate and raising your lactate threshold.

Another key benefit of strength training is maximum force exertion. Simply put, strength and speed are interconnected when it comes to cycling: the stronger your muscles are, the easier it is to pedal a bike. This much seems logical. This can increase your RPM drastically without requiring you to sweat out a greater force exertion on your bike, and allow you to bike faster.

Lastly, by strengthening your muscles, you're strengthening your tendons. Tendons are delicate parts of the body—they are the most common spot for muscle tears, often caused by intense sprinting or sudden acceleration. This risk can be greatly reduced by simply strengthening those muscles. Muscle imbalances pose the same risk; a weak upper body can detract from a strong lower body, or even two muscles next to each other might work against one another if they're not at the same levels of strength.

The purpose of strength training, in relation to the sport of cycling, is ultimately to increase your RPM. This means that, rather than focus on the size of one's muscles, it's more effective to work on their synchronization, and improve the central nervous system's ability to conform each to work in harmony.

Even if you don't want to build up muscle mass— even if your goal is to burn fat and tone up your body without looking like the World's Strongest Man—you should workout at the gym from time to time. Most cyclists and runners actually don't work out their legs at the gym nearly as much as you might think; they work on their core muscles, because their strength comes from a strong centralized position. Slouching is bad; firmness is good.

Strength training is also good for a number of other reasons. Studies have proven that strength training discernibly improves performance times during cycling tournaments, as well as help economize your oxygen usage levels and improve your stamina. And it can also help you spring to the finish line by giving your muscles more strength to finish strong.

That's why squats, dead lifts and bench presses are good mainstays for any cyclist at least some of the time. Winter makes for ideal gym time; the benefits and opportunity are clear.

First, though, we should go over the main muscles that we're going to be using when working out and cycling.

Muscles We Use

Yes, cycling requires leg muscles. But which ones, exactly, are being employed? Let's take a look:

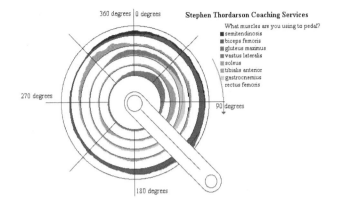

The above image is courtesy of Stephen Thordarson, and illustrates which specific leg muscles are being used during each step of a pedaling motion. As is obvious, the downward pushing gesture is what uses the most energy, and our "*biceps femoris*" (also known as hamstrings) are the heavy lifters in cycling.

This is relevant for a few reasons, but the most important one for us right now is that, because our hamstrings are the ones doing the most work, our hip muscles must necessarily be strong to help push them down. This dispels the myth that some cyclists worry that their knees will become weak because of all the external pressure cycling demands. Our knees shouldn't be doing as much work as our hamstrings—this is easier to achieve when you're pedaling while standing, because you can really throw your weight down.

Other muscles are important, too. The soleus and gastrocnemius—our inner and outer calves, respectively—play a huge role in the downward and upward motions as well, as you can see their contribution closer to the middle of the circle.

Glutes, too, are important for balance, especially when standing while pedaling, which works totally different muscles than the sitting position does.

So, What Exercises Work?

Exercises are necessary for a number of reasons—they help keep our muscles under pressure when we're not cycling, and they keep them strong in preparation for long hauls on the road. It's also key to keep muscles strong to avoid injuries and muscle aches, which can pop up when we put too much of a single stress on our bodies. Literally, we need to flex our muscles every once in a while to keep in good shape.

In truth, there are dozens of different exercises that fitness experts recommend for cyclists. We're going to focus on strength exercises right now, which are shooting for core muscles in the center of the body—things like bench presses and dead lifts. But we'll also touch on some leg workouts, because, after all, you need to keep them in shape if you're going to be cycling day in and day out.

There are general strength exercises, which are mostly aerobic and flex core muscles (presses, extensions and lunges); leg workouts, which are essential for keeping fit legs for strong starts and uphill races; joint exercises, which focus on soothing and strengthening pained joints like ankles and knees; and heavy-duty gym workouts, like squats and dead lifts, which are very similar to what non-runners do at the gym for overall core strength.

For a healthy and balanced regimen, it's a good idea to cycle through workouts (no pun intended), and focus on different parts of the body in different months.

Strength Exercises – At Home

I'm going to start with options for strengthening your core muscles at home. You probably can do these right now; you don't even need to leave your bedroom to do them.

A very basic start for runners, swimmers, cyclists—heck, athletes of all sorts, really—is the **lunge**. A proper lunge is done by simply taking one step forward with one leg until your knee is bent at 90 degrees. You'll stress your hamstrings, glutes and quads with this one, which is why it's so universally revered. If you really want a challenge, add some weight—a dumbbell over your head or horizontally from your outstretched arms, parallel to the floor, can add tremendous advantages.

Another good one is the **plank**. This is often enjoyed by people who want to do as little movement as possible (maybe you have a small room?) but want to maximize their energy output. Just get down into a modified push-up position with your elbows and palms flat on the ground parallel from one another. Now stay there as long as you can—usually about 20 seconds is a good start, but pros can stick it out for up to a full minute. This is a solid workout for your arms, quads and abs.

Lastly, I like to recommend cyclists do **scorpions** as well. If you're unfamiliar (it's a less popular workout, so pardon my explanation), it begins in the elevated push-up position, but with your feet perched up upon a short bench. Now raise your *right* knee to your *left* shoulder as quickly and as far as you can reach, and swiftly pull it back in reverse and try to touch your right *shoulder* with your same right *foot* around your back. You'll look sort of like a scorpion, and suddenly the name will make sense. Be careful not to swing your legs around too unwieldy-like, and maintain control while repeating it for 30 seconds before switching legs. The bonus to this one is you get a good stretch out of it, and look pretty flipping cool while you're at it.

Other traditional core workouts, like crunches and sit-ups, are also recommended to round off a solid core.

Strength Exercises – At The Gym

Now let's get serious. Get a gym membership and hit the place up at least two or three times a week. You can do any of the above exercises here—lunges and planks are common (scorpions less so because of how frankly ridiculous they look, but hey, give them a shot)—but you should definitely focus on core exercises involving heavy weights, too.

One of the most common cyclist exercises are **dead lifts**. They're usually done with a barbell (but modifications have been tried with dumbbells and kettlebells, and that works well also), and involve you standing with the weight freely sitting on the ground in front of you. You have to structure your body properly to get this right—bend over with your legs relatively straight, grab the weight, and smoothly pull the weight up using your back muscles, flutes and hamstrings. Try to keep your body as controlled and stiff as possible.

Next, a personal favorite: **squats**, in pretty much any variation you choose. Some stronger people prefer to add weights, but that's optional. Start by raising your arms parallel to the floor while straightening your back as much as possible. Then focus all of your weight on your heels and squat down until your butt is lower than or level with your knees. This is the perfect workout for your glutes, calves and hamstrings, and if you add weights (like a barbell over your shoulders) then your arms, shoulders and abs get to see some action also.

Lastly, the good old fashioned **bench press** is as good a standby as any. If you're unfamiliar, it's the most basic strength weight lifting exercise there is: lie on a bench, set your weight on the bar and, if you're new, grab a friend to watch over you. (It's easy for your hands to get sweaty, and you don't want to drop all that weight... right above your head.) This is a good workout for shoulders and chest muscles—it may seem counterintuitive for cyclists, but I maintain that if you can hold a barbell firmly over your head, it will make gripping the handlebars of your bike seem like a breeze. A bit silly perhaps, but let's remember that we're going for well-rounded bodies, and the biggest benefit to bench presses is that they work a multitude of upper body muscles all at once, from our arms to our abs and shoulders.

A Cyclist's Strongest Leg Exercises

I'll stress again that no cyclist will exercise exclusively his or her legs; everyone wants a strong amount of all-around strength, even if cycling does demand a lot from our legs. That said, it's important to keep them up to scratch—most of these exercises are good for leg strength but bad for overall strength. Several of these targeted muscles can also be strengthened in other workouts outlined above, but we'll go through them anyway.

If you're at the gym, try to grab ahold of the **hamstring curl** machine. That's the one where you lie flat on your stomach and bend your knees to use your hamstrings to raise up weights you set on the left-hand side of the machine. It's a good one for building pretty exclusively the single most important cycling muscle we have, even if its scope for the rest of our bodies is a bit limited.

While on the topic of hamstrings, I'd also recommend **hamstring push-ups**. They're not often utilized—possibly because they're frankly quite hard. To do one, lie on your back with your feet slightly elevated, either from resting atop of a chair or placing your knees over a small exercise ball so your feet still touch the ground. Then lift one leg straight up and do effectively a push-up with your remaining leg, raising your butt off the ground and straightening your back, then lowering your butt to the ground without touching it—just like you would in a push-up. It's a solid workout for hamstrings and glutes, and actually vaguely resembles a pedaling motion.

I've also always really liked **calf raises**, though they are again very muscle-specific. But they're also quite quick, and easy to do at home—provided you have a set of stairs. Simply hang your heels off a step and drop them a tad before lifting them up as far as you can go, while balancing only on your toes. Hold that position for a few seconds before slowly lowering yourself back to the start. If you go too fast, you won't feel the burn in your calves, which means you're doing it wrong. If it still feels too easy, try it while balancing on one leg.

In general, I will stress, these leg exercises can be easily folded into other workouts. The leg curl machine, for example, which demands you sit in a chair and bend your legs downward, is decent enough, but you get a similar workout by focusing on dead lifts—the latter of which also work out a heck of a lot more parts of your body. What I like about these three is that they take a relatively short amount of time and work strikingly crucial muscles in our legs that cyclists will need to rely on every day.

Words of Workout Warning

If you're not used to spending time at the gym, I'd like to stress a few final key points:

1. **Do not** push yourself harder than you think you can go—the key to improvement is knowing your limits first, and pushing yourself second.

2. **Do not** rush yourself—most workouts require you to go slowly and put as much stress on your muscles as possible, in order to grow them. If you're pressed for time, work multiple joints at once. Single-joint exercises simply aren't as time-efficient as multi-joint exercises. Squats, for example, are great multi-joint exercises that work hips, knees and ankles. This is both a time-saver and a great alleviator of possible injuries.

3. **Do** focus on your whole body—don't focus on legs alone, because that leads to physical imbalance and can actual cause muscle strains quickly. But even within a part of your body (for example, your legs), you don't want to create any imbalances that could lead to a strain. A good example are the lateral quads next to your medial quads—commonly, lateral quads, on the

outside of the thigh, can become much stronger compared to the medials inside the knee, leading to a knee injury.

4. Despite what I just wrote as the number three point, **do** focus on "prime mover" muscles. These are your main cycling muscles—hamstrings, quads and glutes. Ultimately, these are the muscles that matter.

5. **Don't** ignore your core muscles, including your lower back and abs. Climbing hills require core muscles to pull our handlebars and control pedal movement simultaneously. Cores are, quite literally, at the center of all our movements.

6. **Do** try to mimic biking positions with weight exercises. This will help encourage muscle memory when the time comes to replicating your weight lifting on the bike itself. For lifts, when applicable, place your feet about as wide as they would be on your bike. The same goes for the distance and positioning of your hands and arms.

7. **Don't** stick with the same routine over and over again. As a race approaches, if that's what you're training for, change up your weight lifting routine to encourage strong

road racing. Don't worry about time spent in the gym or overall endurance, and focus instead on beefing up your necessary cycling muscles.

Going Through the Phases

On the heels of that last word of warning: there are three phases to strength training, and each should be distinct. This isn't just going to the gym, doing some workouts, getting tired and going home, thinking you're simply ready to hop on the bike and go. This is deliberate training with specific targets in individual sections.

Transparent credit goes to expert cycling trainer Peter Friel for developing this methodology unequivocally—for a more in-depth and thorough approach to cycling fitness, including very precise targets at a high-intensity level, his "Cyclist's Training Bible" is among the best books on the subject.

The first stage is called the "**anatomical adaptation**" period, wherein you have to change your muscles to adapt to weight lifting, instead of pure cardio. You'll need to cast a wide net of muscular activity during this stage, in order to spruce up all your muscles into a stronger condition: the goal is overall improved body strength, rather than focusing on any particular set of muscles. During this first stage, strength machines and free weights are useful, combined into a speedy circuit training regimen to add an element of aerobics and constant movement to an otherwise purely strength-based routine.

The second stage is dubbed the "**maximum transition**" phase, where you transition from all-around body strength into maximum weight loads. You should focus on low reps and heavier loads, and this is where you might begin to focus more on cycling-specific muscles, such as your glutes, quads and core, rather than shoulders and arms.

The goal of the maximum transition phase is to teach your nervous system to use a larger net of muscle fibers in unison. Don't take any risks—as noted above, going slowly and according to your own personal strength is crucial when it comes to weight lifting. Never push above your own limits, but reach them head-on, and as soon as you do you should feel free to add a little more weight as time goes by.

The third stage is known as "**strength maintenance**", and, again, has a fairly self-explanatory title. Rather than building muscles any larger, you want to maintain your level of muscle mass and strength, enabling it for the moment you need it (e.g. a race). The older you are, the more importance this third stage is, because muscles deteriorate at a faster pace over the age of 40.

Final Thoughts: Work it Out

Overall, once you've been to the gym a few times, you'll get into the swing of things. If you can't afford a membership, or just prefer the comfort of your own home, then do what you can—focus on lunges and planks, and you'll still notice improvement in your speed and strength on the bike.

If you do find yourself at the gym regularly, and you are working out hard, supplement your strength training with HIIT workouts on the bike machines instead of longer leisurely 20-minute routines. A little HIIT at the end of a series of squats and dead lifts may have you feeling faint, but damned if you won't feel like you've accomplished something for the week.

Chapter 6
Welcome To Cycling 2.0 (Gadgets, Apps & More)

Getting strong and healthy is one hard, but it's even harder to do alone. Sometimes, it helps to have a little help by your side, be it a personal trainer, onlookers at the gym or a little device strapped to your handlebars shouting virtual words of encouragement.

I find whenever I buy a new toy, I'm immediately excited to use it. Buying new running shoes inspires me to run if I've been in a rut lately; if biking feels stale, and you want to find motivation to hop back in the saddle, then a new gadget might just be the answer.

We're going to diverge from talking about HIIT and muscle-building for a bit and discuss the myriad of bike tech that exists in the world. This will be a brisk chapter, but a worthy one for hobbyists and serious commuters—every year, new technology comes out, and the developments are consistently fascinating.

If you're reading this in 2016 or later, I apologize—some of this might be already outdated!

Awesome Cycling Gadgets

Sure, there are the obvious gadgets—, like a Garmin GPS or *"smart watch"* or cycle computer to record speeds and distances. These types of technology will never go away.

Instead let's talk about some lesser-known gadgets, like **bicycle turn signals.** If you're feeling like raising your arms up and out is too much work (or too hazardous; left turns always wig me out versus oncoming traffic, personally), then consider any number of options for adding turn signals. Some are wirelessly controlled orange arrows you strap on the back, powered by tiny LED light bulbs; others are already incorporated into premade handlebars that double as GPS trackers and turn-by-turn navigation sensors (specifically by a company called Helios, and they look awesome for $200).

Another fun item growing in popularity are *"**boom box bottles**."* I've never found cycling with earbuds to be a safe idea, and this is an ideal solution—a Bluetooth-enabled speaker system that detects your smartphone, fits into your water bottle holder and blasts music at a pretty decent quality. Some also have microphones so you can chat if you receive any incoming calls.

There are also a few brilliant safety gadgets out there that I cannot endorse enough. One is an item called **BikeSpike**, which—while currently limited in scope to the US, EU, Australia and Japan—combines GPS and cellular technology to track your bike at all times. You can even set up "*safety zones*" that you don't want to see your bike leave (for example, city limits or your local neighborhood), and will let you know via your smartphone whether your bike has gone beyond the zone. It also alerts you if someone is messing with your bike, although I can't speak to how easily it's triggered if someone merely parks next to you on the same rack and accidentally bumps you.

The other great safety measure that exists now is the **ICEdot Crash Sensor**, a very specific unit that attaches itself to your helmet and sends alerts to pre-arranged contacts in case of a collision. If you're worried about false alarms, know that the sensor starts with a countdown once it believes an accident has occurred—you can disable the countdown quickly if it's made a mistake, otherwise let the countdown run down and your GPS coordinates will be released. It's ingenious, really, and can significantly help a cycling community ever troubled by rogue potholes and flippant taxi drivers.

The last type of gadget I'm especially fond of is the **generator**. This is very new technology and probably won't fully be realized for another 10 years, but it makes complete sense—if we can create turbine-like energy by cycling, why don't we power our own devices that way? There are a few items on the market that fill this niche. Siva Cycle sells something called the *"Atom"* which attaches to your bike's axel and charges any device with a USB port. (Or, if you don't want to bring your device, you can charge a detachable battery pack in its stead; the pack comes free with the generator purchase.) It's new technology, but costs only $100, which isn't too bad.

Killer Cycling Apps

Even if you don't grab one of those handlebar smartphone holders, you can still zip up your smartphone in a jacket pocket and take it along for the ride to review your stats later, or whip it out in case of emergencies.

There's no shortage of GPS-style cycling trackers. **Cyclemeter**, **Cycle Tracker**, **Cycle Watch** and **Map My Ride** are all great options—some of which cost a little money, and vary in terms of what they offer, but all will calculate your speed and distance effectively. Cyclemeter tends to get featured on the most "top 10" lists because of its simplified design and ability to accurately record heart rates and elevation.

Strava has become renowned in the fitness world for its sociability and is free, with hookups to

Facebook and Twitter to make your bicycling hobby a competitive one, even if you're riding solo.

But there are a few other apps that don't track speed and distance, also worth a look. One fantastic one is **Bike Repair**, a one-stop app with dozens of photos and instructions on how to mend something gone awry with your bike. It costs $2.99, but you'll immediately make that money back the first time you learn how to change your own tire instead of paying someone $10 to do it. **Bike Doctor** is similar to Bike Repair, but a little cheaper ($2.79) and is a strong up-and-comer in the industry.

Another handy one is **Size My Bike**, although if you already know what size bike you should be riding it's probably a bit redundant. Still, you can learn a lot about your own personal morphology and learn about all the different types of mountain and road bikes that are best suited to your body type.

But the mother-lode of all biking apps has got to be **Coach My Ride**, which brings us back to why you're reading this book at all—fitness training. Coach offers more than 100 cycling workouts of varying difficulties, including high-intensity interval training courses. There are regimens based on distance, speed and heart rate, and include endurance rides, cadence changes and ramp-ups, climbing strength intervals and efficiency, and muscular endurance.

At $4.99 it may seem pricier than most apps, but the bundle of illumination you get with it is unbeatable.

No Substitute for Drive

Of course, none of these apps can get you out on a bike any better than honest drive and determination. A lot of gadgets and apps are a bit silly, and not strictly necessary—but the good part is that, in the end, these new technologies are totally optional. Hobbyists can embrace the oncoming changes while purists can cycle alone on the open road, sans distractions. But to know the options exist is always important.

Chapter 7
Supplements & Proper Diet Will Take You Far (Don't Miss Out On This!)

By this point, you might have tried some HIIT workouts. Maybe you've even done interval training before. And maybe you commute every day to work for 30 minutes each way. But you might not have that ideal slender cyclist's body, and you're wondering, Why?

That's because you've got to not just work like a cyclist, but eat like one, too.

There's no secret to the fact that more vegetables and protein, and fewer processed carbs like sugars and breads, are the key to not only a healthy diet but also a healthy mind and fit body.

Some dieticians will recommend eating well under the average recommended daily calorie count—which is 2,000 calories, give or take 500 depending on your age and size.

But bodybuilders and people who want to carve out larger muscles typically need closer to 3,000 calories a day, most of which should be protein and healthy natural fats to fuel their growing muscles.

Though the two might seem contradictory at first, they overlap quite clearly. It all depends on your own personal goals.

Before anything else, you've got to understand (if you don't already) the power of protein. Protein helps repair muscle tissue after it's been abused by weight lifting or heavy-duty cycling. You can find protein most anywhere in formerly living things; it's a major component of every type of meat, including chicken, beef, fish and lamb, as well as any meat byproduct, like milk, cheese or eggs. You might also find trace amounts of protein in nuts, potatoes and legumes, but their ratios are smaller compared to the amount of fat or carbohydrates, so they're less ideal.

Weight lifters need to consume a tremendous amount of protein—think eggs for breakfast, meat-heavy dishes the rest of the day. That's not always healthy. You might find yourself bloating early in the day, or feeling full even when you haven't even approached your recommended daily limit of calories. Besides, it can also be prohibitively expensive to eat only the finest lean chicken all the time—and once you start settling for cheaper beef cuts, you're taking in as much fat as protein.

So what's the solution?

Enter the best friend to cyclists, runners and bodybuilders alike: protein powder.

Most people who are looking for stronger muscles will often turn to protein supplements, including many cyclists who find them personally advantageous and filling. Powders are mixed into milkshakes and provide necessary doses of protein without forcing on you all the myriad other calories and carbs that most foods contain.

A common staple among bodybuilders are supplement powders like whey powder, which is a dense protein extracted from cheese curds. Whey powder is convenient because it consistently provides amino acids (which contribute to the building of muscle mass) and will absorb faster into your body than proteins from meats.

Here's the thing, though. A lot of books—especially eBooks—will try to sell you on one particular brand of protein powder. I think that's nonsense. I'm not in the business of free advertising for any company—this is an unbiased book for your own good.

Many powders are sold online, but look for a protein powder featuring whey if you want more pure protein and less lactose and fat. It might be a bit more expensive, but the gains will be more noticeable. If you want the purest form of whey, aim for whey protein concentrate.

Cyclists should do well to avoid mass gainers, because they're often blended with fat and carbs as well as proteins—ideal for bodybuilders and people who want to gain weight, but less so for cyclists and runners. Anything between one and five grams of carbs and fat is common, versus roughly 20 or 30 grams of protein.

You should also make sure that your protein is made only from the best quality proteins out there. The fewer ingredients the powders have, the better—that means fewer additives like flavor enhancers (vanilla and chocolate are common—come on, people, it's not a *real* milkshake) that will only pump up the calorie count without adding any health benefits. Less chemical processing is also better for firmer results.

You'll be faced with three different types of proteins to choose from: concentrate, casein (pronounced *case*-een) or isolate. All of them are good in different ways, and which you choose should depend on the rest of your diet and your personal fitness goals. Some people enjoy all three; while that's the most extreme you should go (but not uncommon), enjoying one or two per day might be easier to start off with.

We'll start with **protein concentrate** offers a heavy dosage of protein with often very few extra additives. It is the most moderately absorbed of the three powders, and, alone, it can cover up to 85 percent of a regular human's recommended daily dose of protein.

Casein, on the other hand, has a much longer digestion period, making it ideal as a snack after dinner. Because it takes several hours to absorb into your body, it's a terrific booster for while you're sleeping, and can maximize your protein intake by a lot.

Protein isolate is the last of the bunch, and gets absorbed into your body at a very quick rate. Because of this, it's best consumed immediately after working out, so that it can act on your weakened and stressed muscles as quickly as possible.

Take It to the Limit—But Don't Exceed It

I'd like to spread a few words of caution that should follow any attempt at physical transformation, especially when it comes to stuff you're freely putting inside your own body: don't be afraid to be particular.

Remember, you're putting this stuff in your mouth, and it's also getting digested through your stomach and out your rear. This goes inside of you. Don't mess with that privilege. Never buy suspiciously cheap or new products that claim to have all the answers—the side effects may very well be not worth it.

To play it safe, always opt for protein powders with solid reviews and a long-standing history of consumer satisfaction. No gamble is worth the risk when it comes to your own body.

Flashy ads and lots of hype are also telltale signs of warning. Anything offering immediate results, melting fat or quick muscles with suspicious *"before and after"* photos should be examined with a very strict eye. These companies know how desperate consumers get for quick and easy results.

Lastly, you'll have to start counting calories. Be aware of how much protein you're putting in yourself and be careful not to exceed those limits. The chemical process of absorbing protein is such that they're only helpful up until a certain point. Our bodies are limited things, and can't work to an infinite degree.

Specifically, our muscles are unable to handle protein faster than they already do. In other words, just because you're eating more protein doesn't mean it's all going to building your muscles—even if you eat 3,000 calories of protein every day, you're not going to *use* 3,000 calories of protein in a single day, so the excess will actually be stored as fat. Stick with the regular dose of protein and shake intake—just because you're ingesting more, doesn't mean you'll get more protein. There's a natural speed at which these things work, and it isn't less than a few months.

If truth be told (and nobody likes hearing this, but it's true), many athletes get their daily doses of protein simply by eating normal foods—not supplement, shakes or anything. Simply eating yogurt for breakfast, a light chicken salad for lunch and turkey dinner with potatoes and veggies can be enough protein to handle common daily workouts. When tofu's not enough, vegetarians and vegans find protein shakes particularly useful, but it's not necessary for most people.

So even though extra protein can be helpful, it's always a good idea to keep an eye on exactly how much you're taking in and track your results every day. Check your goals and work towards them, and never feel like you need to engage in something or eat something you don't want to. Most importantly, always remember your limits.

Conclusion
Are You Ready To Get Moving? Let's Do It!

Look—I don't know why you ride your bike. Maybe you do it to stay in shape, maybe because it's cheaper than owning a car. Maybe you just genuinely enjoy riding the thing. Or maybe you started as a kid, and riding a bike makes you feel young again. Maybe you're concerned about your environmental footprint and want to avoid using as much gas for the benefit of future generations.

There are a thousand reasons to ride a bike, and a thousand more come up that you might never have realized. I only started biking to work because it was cheaper than taking the bus and faster than walking. I didn't care much about the environment or the athleticism.

But those things do exist, because our society is not a bubble. Actions have multiple reactions. And, in this case, that's a good thing.

The fact of the matter is, it doesn't matter why you started riding your bike. You're getting fit, saving money and supporting green initiatives whether you like it or not, simply by biking as much as you do.

The question isn't, *"Why bike?"* You know the answers.

The question is, rather: *"How to maximize the biking experience?"*

If you're going to do it anyway, do it right. Do it the best that you can. If you bike to save money, then embrace the plethora other reasons, like fitness, by embracing the HIIT program and watching your weight. Make your biking lifestyle easier by strengthening your muscles and trimming down your fat.

The best part is that this isn't a lifestyle change—you've already made the major change when you decided to bike around more often.

Getting in better shape has its own benefits—heart health, strong bone marrow, decreased likelihood of senility, personal stamina, weight loss—you don't need me to list them all. (I don't think I even could.)

Combining the two worlds can bring together a whole new world of personal growth, happiness and clarity of mind.

But more important than any of that is how getting in better shape can improve your pre-existing cycling lifestyle. Even if you're already in fine shape and eat well, don't you want to cycle easier? Have better control over the bike? Feel safer on the road in the thick of traffic?

In short: don't you want to tackle that hill without being out of breath at the top?

When I started my own personal journey just over a year ago, I wasn't expecting much by way of results. I didn't want to change my lifestyle habits too much. I didn't start downing protein powder shakes or doing crunches in my spare time.

All I did was start out by trying HIIT. Once I had tackled that hurdle, going to the gym in the winter seemed like an ideal complement—I could still practice HIIT and work out similar muscles at the same time. Then, of course, I realized that simply working out my muscles without attention to my diet was foolhardy.

This stuff doesn't need to come at you all at once— start somewhere and realize where else benefits may come from. Take your time, go at your own pace, and never let anyone tell you otherwise.

And who knows? Maybe next year you can handle that uphill battle in just a single breath.

Preview Of "Buddhism For Beginners! - The Ultimate Guide To Incorporate Buddhism Into Your Life – A Buddhism Approach For More Energy, Focus, And Inner Peace"

Introduction
Buddhism CAN Change Your Life, Did You Know That?

There's a common misconception that Buddhism is somehow *harder* than Christianity. Think about Christianity: it's easy, right? So, if someone alien were to ask you to describe Christianity, what would you say to them?

Would you describe the imagery of Catholicism, the relevance of the Virgin Mary and emphasis on confessions before God?

Would you talk about the evolution of Protestantism, starting with Martin Luther and how Christianity aims to guide people to be more like Jesus Christ in their actions?

Would you start even further back, all the way back to the writing of the Bible? Before or after the Old Testament? To be truly accurate you'd have to include Abraham and Isaac, and explain most of Judaism while you're at it.

Would you talk about Episcopalians? The United Church? The Westboro Baptist Church? Anglicans? Jehovah's Witnesses? Gospel choirs? The Crusades?

In other words: where do you start, and where do you end?

The fact is that all religions are extremely complex, and Buddhism is no different. Buddhism can't be boiled down into a single phrase: "It's about achieving a Zen understanding of the world, and feeling at peace"—that only begins to describe some of the complexities of a proper Buddhist lifestyle.

But that doesn't mean that Buddhism is difficult to learn. That's why I'm writing this book. I want to help you understand Buddhism from a ground-level, from a totally introductory standpoint, so you can take from it what you'd like. This book isn't meant to convert you to any religion (everyone knows that, as far as conversions go, Buddhists are probably the least likely), but it instead aims to guide you towards understanding what has been the dominant eastern religion for over 2,000 years.

Buddhism isn't alone in this respect—there's divergence with Hinduism, Taoism and Japanese Zen philosophy. They're roughly similar in the way that Judaism, Christianity and Islam are similar—

which they are, actually, because they're all based on the same original stories of Abraham and Isaac, and all deify a supremely powerful being, just in different forms. (The Jewish God was later split into three—the Father, the Son and the Holy Spirit—and Muslims interpreted Him as Allah—but He's actually the same guy in every instance.)

Similarly, there are a myriad forms of Buddhism: Mahayana, Theravada, Cheontae, Zen, Nichiren, Shingon... the list goes on.

And, in fact, Buddhism shares many moral and ethical similarities with Christianity and Judaism. Pretty much every religion, at the end of the day, advocates being a good person, doing good deeds, not committing crimes and helping others. In all respects, education and wisdom is revered over all. Buddhism is much the same. Consider this quote: "Drop by drop is the water pot filled. Likewise, the wise man, gathering it little by little, fills himself with good."

Literally any religious figure could have gotten away with saying that. But you know what? It was the original Buddha.

In order to get the most out of Buddhism and help your day-to-day life, we're not going to focus on the little differences between Buddhism sects. I'll introduce them to you in the first two chapters, along with what Buddhism teaches and what the religion is all about *in a nutshell*, because it's important to grasp the key concepts if you want to understand how to implement it in your life. Then we'll discuss what Buddhism teaches us on a practical level, dealing with subjects such as living in the present moment, the power of meditation and yoga (which are, actually, more similar than you might believe) and how the age-old concept of karma—including rebirth and how good deeds beget happiness—can help guide us through everyday life, even if we don't believe it literally.

The fact is, like all religions, it is not only difficult but extremely dangerous to follow it 100 percent. We've come to a point as a global society—with the ease of access to information that the internet has provided, and now that we can hear so many different viewpoints, philosophies and religious beliefs—that individualizing is becoming important and popular. There's a reason that every religion is seeing smaller and smaller numbers each year. Churches report lower attendance records, and most Jews identify more with the secular Woody Allen and Jerry Seinfeld than the ancient wise man Rabbi Hillel.

And more than that, we're learning that it's not a crime to dip into multiple religions. You can turn the other cheek like Jesus says, and also celebrate Passover with your Jewish friends. We've successfully convinced ourselves that, as long as we are true and decent people, which God we believe in matters less than how we live our lives.

And you know what? That's what Buddhism teaches us.

Buddhism is a *nontheistic* religion. That means Buddhists don't believe in a One Almighty God. Buddhists instead try to find inner peace, within themselves, not relying on an outside being to teach them. It is a religion based on self-importance, self-respect and, perhaps most importantly, self-discipline. That makes it easy to adopt certain Buddhist practices into our daily lives. Heck, we do it already, all the time—think of yoga, or mantras, or we repeat to ourselves, or the belief in good and bad karma, or meditation. These are all phrases and acts adopted from Buddhism, which have seeped into our everyday lives and our everyday vocabulary.

When you think of it that way, Buddhism isn't so foreign.

But wait, you might be saying. Back up a second. If there's no God, then who are all those statues of? Who's the big fat laughing guy, and the snarling big-eared one? And who was the original Buddha, if not a God?

And you know what? I'm going to answer all those questions in the upcoming chapters. There are too many questions. Questions are crucial in Buddhism—it's a good thing to ask them. Hopefully, I'll be able to answer as many as I can.

The fact is that Buddhism, as we know it today, has been around for over 2,000 years and has been the foundation of dozens of civilizations—some successful, some now extinct. Buddhist structures, statues and temples are some of the most historically enduring and spiritually meaningful monuments in the world: think of Cambodia's mighty Ankor Wat, a massive temple complex over 1,000-years-old; Borobudur, a magnificent ancient stone pyramid in central Java, Indonesia, that welcome a gorgeous sunrise every morning; the Hill Temple, nestled between vibrant green trees and overlooking the ancient city of Kyoto, Japan; Thailand's Wat Pho, with a famously luxurious-looking reclining Buddha, said to be the birthplace of Thai massage; and South Korea's colorful temples, like Guinsa and Haeinsa, filled with chanting monks and towering stone pagodas.

Buddhism is no joke. It's not a small belief, and it's historically older than our Biblical realities, dating back to the 5th and 6th century BC. There's no excuse to be ignorant of what the eastern half of the world believes, and there's no reason we can't learn from it.

So, for now, put your mind at ease. Put on some soft, meditative music. And let's get started.

Chapter 1
Who the First Buddha Was & What He Taught

There once was a man, around 2,600 years ago, who was born in northern India, in the foothills of the Himalayan mountains, which is now part of southern Nepal. His name was Siddhartha Gautama. Gautama was born into royalty as an opulent young aristocratic prince, with a life surrounded by comfort and luxury.

But Gautama had a problem: he wasn't very happy. It's the age-old story of "money can't buy you happiness," and it doesn't buy Gautama any joy at all. He finds himself confused, restless and constantly questioning of everything. He had a philosophical mind.

So, discouraged by his lifestyle, Gautama left his palace at the age of 29 in search of greater meaning in the world. This was the first time he had left home and witnessed the outside world. He saw the problems of the world for the first time: the sick, the old, the suffering. The naïve prince was eager to learn more about these real-world problems. He started going on more trips outside the palace to interact with people more people who were diseased, vain and dying. These problems depressed him immensely, and he decided to change his lifestyle completely.

He became an ascetic—one who abstains from mortal pleasures. He threw himself into a world devoid of expensive belongings and material wealth, and began begging for alms, pure charity, in the street. His goal was humility.

Eventually someone spotted and recognized him (as a prince, you'd think it wouldn't take too long) and tried to bring him back to the world of royalty. He denied this offer, too, and instead changed course: he began seeking out every great philosophical mind of his time, looking for answers to his problems of happiness.

He went to practice yogic meditation with the masters, and excelled at it to the point of being offered to succeed the masters as a permanent teacher, but Gautama denied this offer, too. He tried a different sort of yoga under a different teacher, and attained a high plateau of meditative consciousness—again, impressed with his determination, the then-master asked him to stay. But Gautama still wasn't satisfied.

He then turned to self-mortification: a deeper kind of humility. He deprived himself of all worldly luxuries, including food. Allegedly eating only a single leaf or nut per day, he nearly starved himself to death. He wanted no part of any world that would continue to offer him luxuries of any sort, including status as a "master" or "king". The very thought of hierarchy put a bad taste in his mouth.

By now he was 35-years-old, and found himself sitting beneath what has today become famous as the Bodhi Tree, now in Bodh Gaya, India, in the distant groves near the Neranjara riverbanks. He fell, nearly unconscious due to starvation, and promised himself he wouldn't wake up until he'd found enlightenment. He then fell into a deep meditative state, and found a previously unimaginable state of clear and thorough consciousness. He began thinking about the world, the universe, the nature of life.

This took 49 days, so the legend goes.

From that point on, he was known as the Buddha—or, later, once more Buddhas start popping up throughout history (and yes, there are at least 28 more; but no, we won't get into all of them in as much detail), he became known as the Supreme Buddha. "Buddha" means, simply, "Awakened One" or "Enlightened One," so the title fits.

What Did He Learn?

It's complicated, even impossible, to know exactly what he thought that night he underwent enlightenment. Certainly, at the very least, he shoved aside asceticism and self-mortification, along with self-indulgence at every level. He essentially created Buddhism as we know it today, and though what exactly that means can be vague, he does provide some helpful guides, which are known as dharma.

He wrote down his newfound doctrine based on what we know as "The Four Noble Truths", through which followers of Buddhism can reach Nirvana. Nirvana is the end goal in Buddhism: it is a state of awesome freedom, total ease of mind and mental mastery. To translate it into religious terms, it's heaven on earth. Anyone can reach a state of mental nirvana through dedication to Buddhism and following the teachings of Gautama.

To be in a state of nirvana means to ignore greed, selfishness, anger and other distracting emotions. It is, in a word, to be emotionally *above* the rest of the world. It sounds a bit haughty, but the idea is this completely carelessness about oneself, a delicate balance between being self-centered and not being egocentric. Nirvana means being altruistic and kind, understanding selflessness enough to know how small you are in the universe, and being okay with that.

According to one story, immediately after waking up from his Enlightenment, the Buddha wasn't sure if he should teach others his dharma. He wasn't sure everyone could handle it: after all, humans are afflicted by greed and ignorance all the time, which is why he had to go through this six-year meditative process to figure it out at all. Buddha told his problem to a friend, who convinced him that at least some people will grasp his meaning. Buddha agreed to have faith, and so the dharma was born into public.

What Does He Teach?

We're going to break down Buddhism really simply for you now, just because, well, this is an eBook, and we have a lot of other topics to touch on. So excuse me as I skip some of the details and sections like the Five Skandhas and Six Realms, which basically explain how to view life, and instead focus on what the Supreme Buddha wants *you* to learn.

The Four Noble Truths

There are four realities to face when you look at the world. The Four Noble Truths were what the Supreme Buddha first taught in his very first sermons to the public, so this is very Buddha-101 appropriate.

The first truth is that *there is suffering in the world*. We may know this phrase as, "Shit happens." Basically, life can be difficult—loved ones get hit by cars, our pets get cancer, we get fired, babies die in the womb, an African child just died as you read this sentence, schools get shot up; even if you avoid all of this, in the best-case scenario, you're going to die one day. Basically, there is pain, strife and difficulty. This is a truth of the world, and the first one we must face in order to achieve enlightenment: even if our own particular lives are mostly okay (i.e. none of the above apply, save for the death bit), the world is a harsh and brutal place. The First Noble Truth tells us that we must mentally face this head-on: think about it. Believe in it. Confront it.

The second truth defines this suffering: *every suffering has a cause*. There are a few causes. One is a craving for something: for respect, for power, for control, for material happiness. The other reasons we suffer are because we are trying to define ourselves as something we are not, or do not want to be; for example, if we're sad but want to be happy, we are trying to redefine ourselves in that moment. We try to unite with experiences in the way that we want to be constantly connected to the outside world, have a past, present and future life, and be successful. Or else we crave the opposite: to not feel sad when we don't want to, or to escape from painful emotions.

The Third Noble Truth is that *your suffering can end*. It is possible, in other words, to remove ourselves from our problems. We can rethink our lives, and redefine our personalities. Once we realize how loosely tied we are to our personalities, we can work on new ones. We don't need to pretend to fit in when we don't. We don't need to impress people we don't get alone with. We could be simpler than that, and focus on affirming ourselves to ourselves alone. We need to remove the cravings from the Second Noble Truth and focus on our real needs.

The fourth and final Noble Truth is *how to end the suffering*. It's a subtle wording difference from number three, but a significant one: while three tells us *that we can* end our suffering, four begins to tell us *how*. The answer is, basically, mindful meditation; in a longer answer, the path to happiness involves what's called **The Eightfold Path**.

The Eightfold Path

The Eightfold Path is crucial to every Buddhist practice, and comprises the Fourth Noble Truth in its entirety. It is the path to enlightenment, true understanding and personal happiness.

At the risk of turning this chapter into an extremely dense introduction, I'm going to go over the Eightfold Path very quickly, in point-form, so as to not overload you all at once.

The Noble Eightfold Path is divided into eight ways to act correctly. They're called the Rights. So remember that when you read Right here, it means Right as in Objectively Correct.

The eight Rights are divided into three sub-sections, including Wisdom, Ethical Conduct and Concentration.

The two filed under *Wisdom* describe a proper Buddhist mental state:

1. **Right View** – Sometimes called "Right Perspective" or "Right Outlook", this can be summed up as the proper way of looking at the nature of things, the way the world exists in its natural form, which can adopt an almost scientific perspective: physics, chemistry and biology all dictate our world.

2. **Right Thought** – Thinking good thoughts will give you a good life. To achieve this you must mentally renounce material goods and think instead about what matters: good deeds, peacekeeping, charity and being kind towards others.

The three steps under *Ethical Conduct* progress this lifestyle into reality:

3. **Right Speech** – So, you've got those good thoughts in your head? Speak them. No lying, no wasteful chitchat, no insults.

4. **Right Action** – Talk is cheap—do good deeds. Don't kill, steal or rape.

5. **Right Livelihood** – Don't make your job an evil one. Don't create weapons, don't trade slaves, don't sell drugs, don't kill people. According to Buddha, the "business of meat" is also a no-no; sorry, butchers.

The last three, under *Concentration*, might be the hardest to achieve:

6. **Right Effort** – This describes preventative measures. If you're leading a true Buddhist life, you will need effort to actively subdue your material and worldly urges. Be mindful of the good that has no yet risen within yourself, and abstain from the evil.

7. **Right Mindfulness** – Also translated as "Right Memory", to be mindful of something means you're keeping it in mind. You should be constantly aware of every

part of your body, in tune with your health and mental state, to continue your other Right ways.

8. **Right Concentration** – Also known as "Right Meditation", this simply defines an ideal meditative state: one aloof from the world, purely tranquil and absorbed by your mental cleanness.

Phew! That about sums it up. Thanks for hanging in there. I know this stuff can get a little dense at times, but, as the Noble Eightfold Path shows, it's actually pretty natural. It's the same basic morality as suggested by Abrahamic religions: think good thoughts, do good deeds, and stay that way.

The big departures in Buddhism come in the specific logic of the religion. The description of the mind and body is different from the Christian conception of the soul. Nirvana is different from heaven. But only in logical terms.

If looked at abstractly, from a bit far away, you'll find that the first of the Four Noble Truths—that there is suffering in the world—is an issue debated and tackled by every major religion in the world. Others might simply chalk it up to the old phrase, "God works in mysterious ways." The big change in Buddhism is that it tries to define that problem and, instead of promoting belief in God or Jesus to save you from such dangers and bring you to heaven, the Supreme Buddha suggests believing in yourself and overcoming these worldly problems while you're still on Earth.

This is by no means a comprehensive analysis—we still haven't gotten to karma, rebirth or the thousands of other little details that create Buddhism. But we'll get there soon.

For now, and in the next chapter, we're going to look at a few variations of Buddhism, and how it's affected the world as we know it.

To check out the rest of "<u>Buddhism For Beginners! - The Ultimate Guide To Incorporate Buddhism Into Your Life – A Buddhism Approach For More Energy, Focus, And Inner Peace</u>", **click here or go to Amazon and look for it right now!**

Ps: You'll find many more books like these under my name, Dominique Francon.

Don't miss them! Here's a short list:

- Buddhism For Beginners
- Meditation For Beginners
- Reiki For Beginners
- Yoga For Beginners

- Running Will Make You FIT
- Cycling HIIT Training

- Paleo Recipe Cookbooks
- Much, much more!

About the Author

Dominique Francon is a significant health connoisseur devoted to helping others get healthy all around the world.

From a very young age, Francon understood the value and potential of leading a healthy lifestyle. And because of her genuine appreciation and enthusiasm for all things health-related, she has dedicated a great deal of time and effort to researching the best of what fitness, nutritional diets and overall wellbeing programs have to offer.

In the beginning, Francon focused on working with people in various gym and sports club settings. Before long she became exceedingly in tune with the health and fitness solutions that had the best results for her clients' issues and goals. But after years of accumulating one health expertise following another, Francon decided she wanted to reach out to even more individuals.

She wanted to help people on a bigger scale. For this reason she resolved to share her extensive knowledge with people through writing and publishing books pertaining to her vast health-related know-how. Currently she has authored books on such cutting-edge topics as paleo cooking, Zen, Yoga, running and cycling.

Francon has a real passion for all the subjects she writes about and she takes the job seriously. She knows self-development is, for a lot of people, as significant as it is for her. But she also knows how tough it is to change one's lifestyle. With this in mind, her aim while writing is to make the concepts and instructions as helpful and accessible to her readers as possible. After all, for her the end objective is improving the lives of others.

Printed in Great Britain
by Amazon.co.uk, Ltd.,
Marston Gate.